Chips and Cheese and Nana's Knees

What Is Alliteration?

Alliteration:
The repetition of a sound at the beginning of two or more words that are near one another

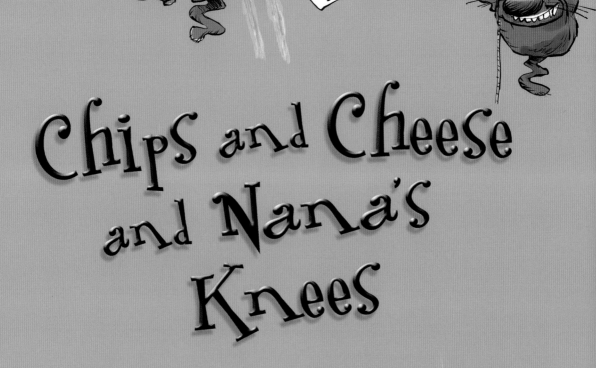

Chips and Cheese and Nana's Knees

What Is Alliteration?

by Brian P. Cleary

illustrations by Martin Goneau

M MILLBROOK PRESS / MINNEAPOLIS

When words are close together and they start with the same sound

it's called **alliteration**, as in, "Frances froze and frowned."

and once you learn about it,
then you'll see it everywhere!

Like, "Lovely lemon lollipops
are likely to be licked."

Or "Petals on the pink petunias peacefully are picked."

These sounds are formed by
letters—some identical,
some not—

See how "Kevin's" starts with K, but C is what starts "cool"?

12

So it's the sounds, not letters, then

that really form this rule.

The same sound is repeated
once or twice or even more,

Who Wants
to Win a
Watermelon?

as in "Fiona found her phone

on Phoebe's kitchen floor."

At times, alliteration makes a sentence sound quite silly,

as in, "The hike with Hank and Mike

Was humid, hot, and hilly."

Or here:

"A knight arrives one night
and knocks upon our door.

He needs a knife so Nan,
his wife, can cut their
cake in four."

Or even "Peter Piper picked up pepperoni pie

When he popped in
the pizza place
he often passes by."

21

as in, "The bride with braids of brown

strung streamers all around."

Or "Brian's brothers
Brad and Brent

have brought
banana bread,

Alliteration's

Seen in **Signs** and **Streets** that might **surround** you.

We calmly cruised the countryside, that dark December day.

FM1 96.7

It's on the news,
your **shirt**, your **shoes**,

SPORTS SPOT LIVE FROM MARTHA'S MARATHON

in talk and
texts and
tweeting.

It packs some punch in poetry

Tonight: Poetry Slam

and always bears repeating!

So what is alliteration?
Do you know?

Alliteration can happen with one letter . . .

Sound	Word	Word	Word
e	eat	eel	even
g	garden	get	grow
l	lake	leaf	love
n	name	near	number
z	zebra	zipper	zoom

. . . two letters . . .

Sound	Word	Word	Word
ch	chain	cheat	chicken
fl	flicker	float	fly
in	indoor	inner	instant
sh	sheet	shower	shovel
tr	train	trick	trot

... or more!

Sound	Word	Word	Word
bla	black	bland	blast
dri	drift	drill	drip
par	parcel	park	party
scr	scream	scroll	scrunch
thr	threat	thrill	throat

Sometimes, different letters can make the same sound!

Sound	Word	Word
c / s	Cindy	south
c / k	cat	kite
g / j	gem	jelly

ABOUT THE AUTHOR AND THE ILLUSTRATOR

BRIAN P. CLEARY is the author of the best-selling Words Are CATegorical® series as well as the many other children's books, including the Math Is CATegorical©, Food Is CATegorical™, Animal Groups Are CATegorical™, and Poetry Adventures series. Mr. Cleary lives in Cleveland, Ohio.

MARTIN GONEAU is the illustrator of the Food Is CATegorical™ and Animal Groups Are CATegorical™ series. Mr. Goneau lives in Trois-Rivières, Québec.

Millbrook Press
A division of Lerner Publishing Group, Inc.
241 First Avenue North
Minneapolis, MN 55401 USA

For reading levels and more information, look up this title at www.lernerbooks.com.

Main body text set in RandumTEMP 35/48. Typeface provided by House Industries.

Library of Congress Cataloging-in-Publication Data

Cleary, Brian P., 1959-
    Chips and cheese and Nana's knees: What is alliteration? / By Brian P. Cleary ; Illustrated by Martin Goneau.
        pages   cm. — (Words Are CATegorical ®)
    ISBN 978-1-4677-2649-8 (lib. bdg. : alk. paper) — ISBN 978-1-4677-6303-5 (EB pdf)
    1. English language—Phonetics—Juvenile literature. 2. English language—Rhyme—Juvenile literature.
3. Alliteration—Juvenile literature. I. Goneau, Martin, illustrator. II. Title.
PE1135.C54 2015
    421'.58—dc3   2014009378

Manufactured in the United States of America
1 — DP — 12/31/14